To **ELISE EMERIE ERYNNE**

From
Good Shepherd UMC Malden, MA USA

Date
Christmas 2020

OK, I Admit It, I'm Afraid

Anthony DeStefano

HARVEST HOUSE PUBLISHERS
EUGENE, OREGON

OK, I Admit It, I'm Afraid

Copyright © 2015 by Anthony DeStefano

Photos compiled by Anthony DeStefano

Published by Harvest House Publishers

Eugene, Oregon 97402

www.harvesthousepublishers.com

978-0-7369-6471-5

Cover design and production by Left Coast Design, Portland, Oregon

Photographs used with permission from the following sources: iStockPhoto, Dollar Photo Club, PhotoDune, and Schmalen Design, Inc.

Digital photo editing by Schmalen Design, Inc.

Printed in China

15 16 17 18 19 20 21 22 23 / LP / 10 9 8 7 6 5 4 3 2 1

This book
is dedicated
to the wonderful
Schmalen family,
Amy, Andy, and
Andy Jr.

OK, I admit it, I'm afraid.

I always try to
pretend that I'm brave,
but when I'm really honest
with myself, I realize that
I'm afraid of practically
everything.

I'm afraid of the dark—

Not just when
the lights are out,
but anytime I can't
see and understand
what's going on
around me.

I'm afraid of storms.

Not just the ones with lightning
and thunder, but any kind
of confrontation.

I'm afraid of things that are bigger than me.

I'm afraid
of things that
are smaller
than me.

I'm afraid of being bullied.

I'm afraid of
not being able to
pay my bills.

I'm afraid of public speaking.

I'm afraid of flying.

I'm afraid of being in crowds.

I'm afraid of being alone.

I'm afraid of failure.

I'm afraid of working hard to succeed.

I'm afraid of doing
anything new—

Or outside my comfort zone.

I'm afraid of rejection.

I'm afraid of facing the truth about myself—

because what I see isn't always so pretty.

I'm afraid of my own bad habits, temptations, and weaknesses—and doing what I have to do to overcome them.

I'm afraid of forgiving people
when they hurt me.

And apologizing when I hurt others.

I'm afraid of being sick—in fact,
I'm a big baby!

I can't even mention how afraid
I am of the "D" word—not just for
myself, but for everyone I love.

And crazy as it sounds, I'm even
afraid of God sometimes.

But I guess the main thing I'm afraid of is that I just don't have what it takes to deal with any of my problems—that I'm not smart enough or strong enough or good enough.

So yes, I admit it, I'm afraid!

And yet, the Bible says in so many different places that I shouldn't be afraid of anything.

Fear not

Be not afraid

Holy Bible

Holy Bible

In fact, it says "be not afraid" or "fear not" over 100 times! How can that be when life is so scary?

I wonder... Is it because God has a plan for me, and He knows what He's doing, even when I don't?

Or that I'm never really alone because
His angels are watching over me?

Or that His grace can give me the power
to do extraordinary things?

Or that He can always pull good
out of bad situations?

Or that I
need to be more grateful
for my blessings and less fearful
of life's uncertainties?

After all, I've made it through all my problems so far. Maybe I'll make it through this one too.

I know all this is true, and yet I'm still afraid! No matter what I think, my emotions always seem to get the better of me.

I end up feeling exhausted and worn-out.

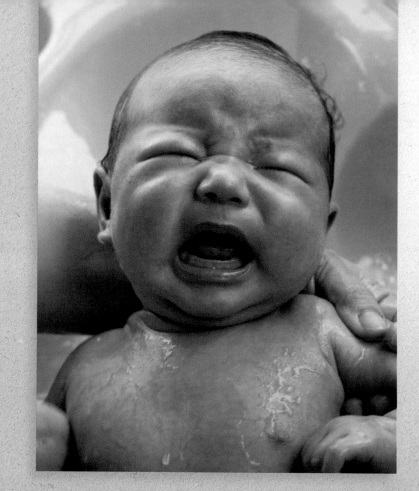

What can I do? Should I just let my fear *wash* over me and drown me?

Or should I, perhaps, do something else?
Should I try to let my fear wash *away*?

When I do that—when I just breathe and allow my emotions to subside...

...I realize that I might not drown after all.
That I'm really standing on a rock—the rock of
FAITH. Not just some passing emotional
"feeling," but my will to believe and
trust the One who created me.

Standing here
alone with God,
knowing full well that
what I have to deal with is beyond my abilities
and control, that I have no power to do anything
on my own, I just listen—really, truly listen.

"What are You trying to tell me?"
I ask God. "What are You
trying to teach me?"

When I push all the other thoughts and feelings out of my head, I always hear the same whispered response: "Don't be afraid. Don't try to understand. Just *take up your cross and follow Me.*

And then, finally, I see a glimmer of hope.

Because deep down in my heart
I know that even though I'm small
and weak and afraid, God isn't.

He's all-knowing,
so there's no
problem He can't
figure out.

He's all-powerful,
so there's no
problem He can't
overcome.

He's all-good, so there's no problem that can really harm me since He wants only what's best for me—in this life and the next.

With God, nothing is impossible. When I'm connected to Him, I'm connected to the power source of the whole universe— and nothing is impossible for me either.

I can fight
and vanquish
every enemy
imaginable.

I can find the strength to go on—
no matter how hard.

I can find all the energy, wisdom, virtue, self-discipline, patience, and love to deal with ALL of my problems.

So from now on, no matter what happens to me, I'm going to make the decision to have faith in God's plan and **DO WHAT I HAVE TO DO!**

Instead of being worried, I'm just going to TRUST.

For once in my life, I'm going to put everything in God's hands. I'm going to give Him every last bit of my fears and doubts and anxieties.